PENGUINS & POLAR BEARS

A Pretty Cool Introduction to the Arctic and Antarctic

Illustrated by Grace Helmer
Written by Alicia Klepeis

LITTLE GESTALTEN

VISITING THE ENDS OF THE WORLD

Did you know that penguins and polar bears never meet? Penguins live in the Antarctic regions in the south and polar bears can only be found in the northern part of the world, the Arctic. Follow their footprints through the book: they'll indicate whether you're up north or down south.

The Paw of a Polar Bear

The Arctic is the world's northernmost region, and includes the north pole and the Arctic Ocean basin. This part of the world is nearly completely covered by water, much of which is frozen in the form of icebergs, glaciers, and sea ice.

The Foot of a Penguin

The Antarctic is the world's southern-most region and includes the south pole and the rocky continent of Antarctica. The Antarctic ice sheet is perhaps its most iconic feature—after all, it's the biggest single piece of ice on Earth!

The Arctic

The Antarctic

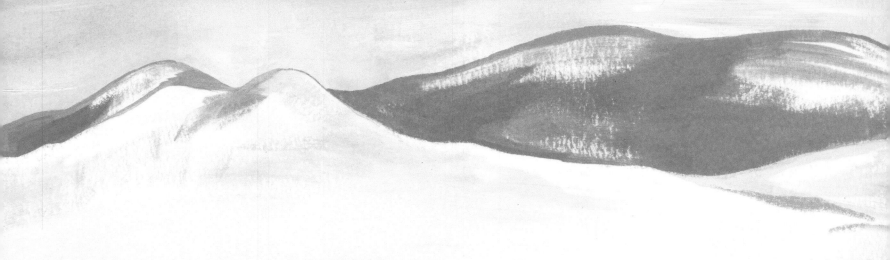

CLOSE YOUR EYES...

Imagine you are going to the ends of the Earth. It's beyond cold. The winds are whipping round you, making your skin feel like it's burning. The frigid air is causing your eyes to water. Snow and ice blanket the landscape. It's blindingly bright.

Only the bravest of explorers have traveled to the Arctic and Antarctic. Their expeditions have taught us much about the plants, animals, and waters of the polar regions. There is so much to discover. Let's go on a journey! You'll need the right gear and plenty of hearty food to keep you healthy and warm as you find out more about these fascinating frozen worlds.

Are you ready to explore? Put on your warmest clothes. Grab a chocolate bar or some dried fruit. Pack your camera and perhaps a set of binoculars. And get ready for some thrilling adventures. It's time to check out the magnificent and mysterious polar regions. You'll learn things you never knew before about the Arctic and Antarctic!

EXPLORER'S PACKING LIST

Exploring the polar regions as an Arctic or Antarctic adventurer takes not just courage, but also the right gear for these extreme environments.

Polar explorers cannot carry all their supplies on their backs. It's common for them to pull their food and gear behind them in a sled. Today's high-tech sleds glide well over rough terrain, ice, and snow. Many are amphibious, which means they can be used when you're crossing water, too. Packed inside could be anything from chocolate bars to rope to an explorer's journal!

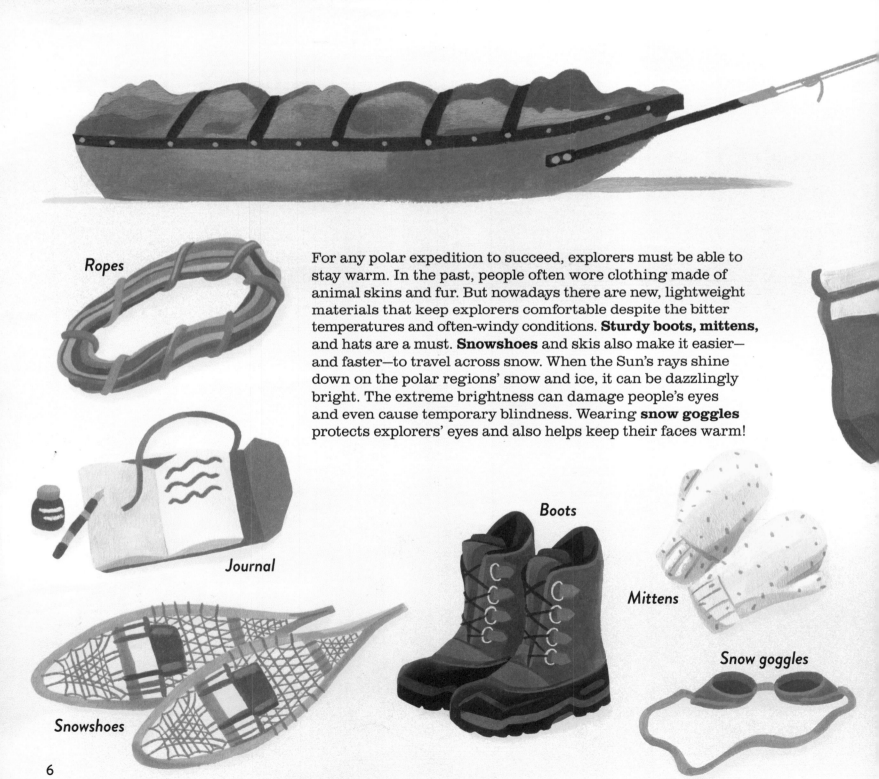

For any polar expedition to succeed, explorers must be able to stay warm. In the past, people often wore clothing made of animal skins and fur. But nowadays there are new, lightweight materials that keep explorers comfortable despite the bitter temperatures and often-windy conditions. **Sturdy boots, mittens, and hats are a must. Snowshoes** and skis also make it easier—and faster—to travel across snow. When the Sun's rays shine down on the polar regions' snow and ice, it can be dazzlingly bright. The extreme brightness can damage people's eyes and even cause temporary blindness. Wearing **snow goggles** protects explorers' eyes and also helps keep their faces warm!

Ropes

Journal

Snowshoes

Boots

Mittens

Snow goggles

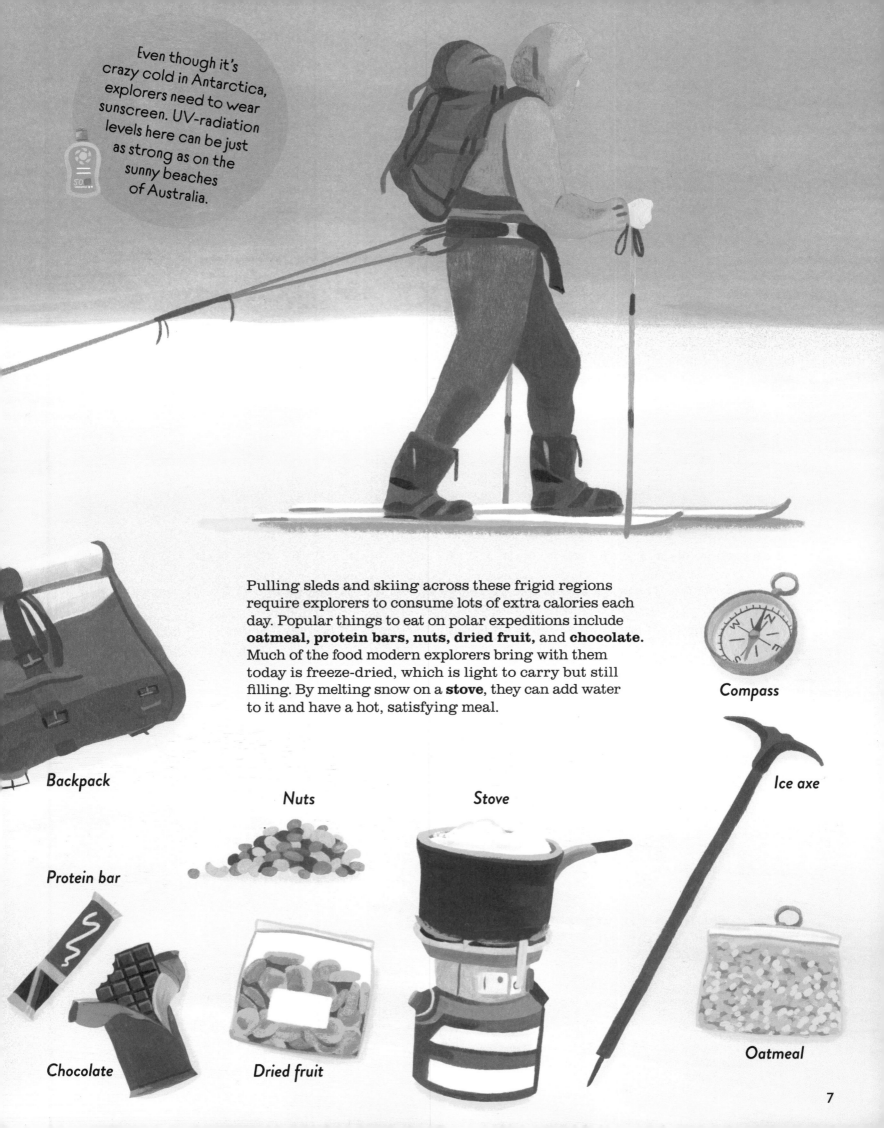

Even though it's crazy cold in Antarctica, explorers need to wear sunscreen. UV-radiation levels here can be just as strong as on the sunny beaches of Australia.

Pulling sleds and skiing across these frigid regions require explorers to consume lots of extra calories each day. Popular things to eat on polar expeditions include **oatmeal, protein bars, nuts, dried fruit,** and **chocolate.** Much of the food modern explorers bring with them today is freeze-dried, which is light to carry but still filling. By melting snow on a **stove**, they can add water to it and have a hot, satisfying meal.

Backpack

Compass

Ice axe

Protein bar

Nuts

Stove

Chocolate

Dried fruit

Oatmeal

BATTLE OF THE BRRR!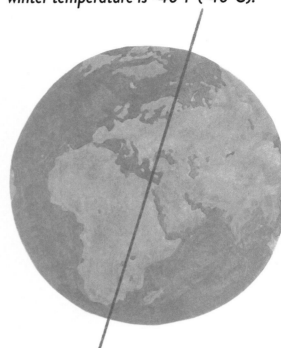

Although both the Arctic and Antarctic have super-cold climates, the Antarctic is the chilly champion.

At the north pole, the average summer temperature is 32°F (0°C) and the average winter temperature is -40°F (-40°C).

The coldest temperatures ever recorded on Earth have been in Antarctica. In 1983, Vostok Station, one of the most remote research stations on the Antarctic continent, measured -128.6°F (-89.2°C)! Can you imagine that? The polar regions basically have two seasons each year: winter and summer. Neither is especially warm. That's because, even in the summer, the sun doesn't rise high enough above the horizon to make temperatures toasty.

It's funny that all of Antarctica and some areas in the Arctic are known as deserts. They aren't the hot, sunny kind, of course. They are considered deserts since very little precipitation occurs there. In fact, some of Antarctica's inner regions only get about two inches (50 millimeters) of precipitation—mostly snow—each year. That's half as much as many parts of the Sahara desert receive! This makes Antarctica the driest continent on Earth.

It's much colder at the south pole. There, the average summer temperature is -18°F (-28.2°C) and the average winter temperature is -76°F (-60°C).

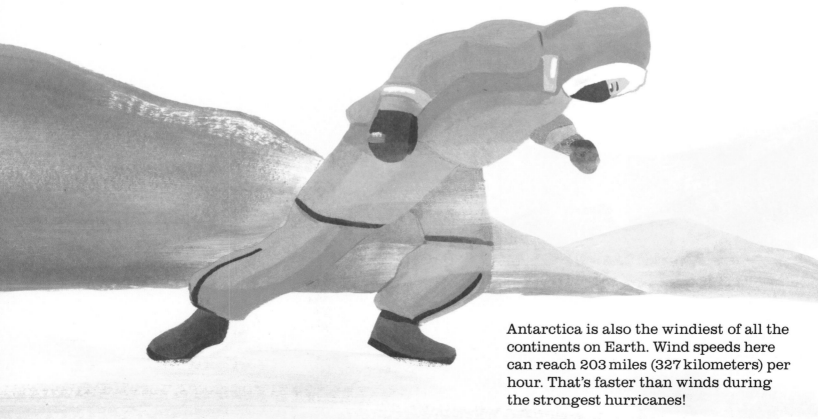

Antarctica is also the windiest of all the continents on Earth. Wind speeds here can reach 203 miles (327 kilometers) per hour. That's faster than winds during the strongest hurricanes!

8

Popular games among children of Inuit communities in the Arctic region include hide-and-seek and tag.

Temperatures don't get as low in the Arctic, which means people can live in many parts of the region. You might think children who go to school in the Arctic always have indoor recess because of the cold climate. Not so! In many Arctic schools, outdoor recess is required unless temperatures reach -58°F (-50°C). Students there better not forget their hats and mittens!

Kids who live in Nunavut, which is one of the most remote areas of the world, in northern Canada, play hockey all year long. They even have games during the periods of 24-hour darkness.

If you throw a cup of hot tea into the air during the polar regions' wintertime, it can turn from a liquid into a solid. The tea becomes tiny ice crystals!

ANTARCTIC ICE SHELVES

Ninety percent of all the ice on Earth is contained in the Antarctic ice sheet! Its landscape is high and dry and dazzlingly bright, with many kinds of ice.

Antarctica is made up of two parts: **East Antarctica** and **West Antarctica**. It is a land of ice, which comes in different forms and shapes. The actual area of Antarctica is always changing due to the melting and freezing of the ice here.

If the Antarctic ice sheet ever melted, sea levels around the world would go up by more than 200 feet (61 meters).

West Antarctica is smaller and contains younger rock (volcanic and sedimentary) that is up to 500 million years old—young in comparison!

Mount Erebus is the world's southernmost volcano. It's located on Ross Island, off the coast of West Antarctica. Still active, Erebus sometimes throws out rock bombs, and also has a lava lake at its summit. Nearby are **fumaroles**—steaming ice towers that release gas and steam, just like the volcano itself.

Fumarole

Antarctica is the highest of the continents. Its average elevation is about 8,200 feet (2,500 meters).

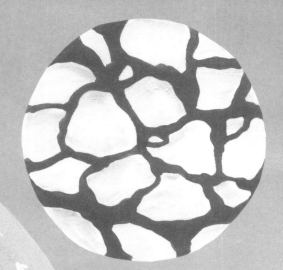

In the winter, the surface waters around the Antarctic continent freeze into a huge ice slab that's 10 feet (three meters) thick. Each summer, the ice slab breaks up into **pack ice** that gradually drifts into the ocean and melts.

East Antarctica is the bigger of the two, about the size of the United States. It is made up of rock that is up to three billion years old in places.

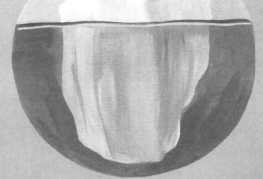

Pack ice can also develop into **icebergs** or **ice floes**.

Mount Erebus

When the ocean around the Antarctic freezes in the winter, it's almost impossible to reach the land.

Circling Antarctica is a heavy stream that separates the ice-cold waters from the water of the warmer oceans.

Two huge **ice sheets** cover more than 97 percent of the Antarctic continent. This ice built up over millions of years as snow got packed down. On average, the ice sheets are 7,086 feet (2,160 meters) thick. That's much taller than the world's biggest skyscrapers, including the Burj Khalifa in Dubai, the Shanghai Tower in China, and One World Trade Center in New York.

ARCTIC ISLANDS 🐾

The environment of the Arctic is very special. Water covers most of the region, but the landscape also includes a variety of landforms.

The **north pole** lies in the center of the **Arctic Ocean**. Much of the Arctic region is covered with ice for most, or even all, of the year. Along the edges of the Arctic Ocean are islands and continents that are largely icy and very cold. You can find water in many different forms here, such as lakes, ice shelves, or glaciers. The icebergs and glaciers in the Arctic make up roughly 20 percent of all the fresh water on Earth. Islands can be found throughout the Arctic, too. Here are some examples:

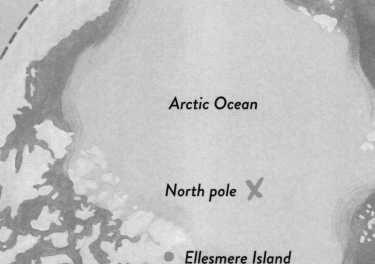

Siberia

Arctic Ocean

North pole ✖

● Ellesmere Island

Ilulissat

Lofoten Islands
Kaskasapakte & Lake Tarfala
Sognefjord

Kaskasapakte is one of the Arctic's many mountains. It stands 6,703 feet (2,043 meters) high in northern Sweden. Glacial ice flows down its slope into **Lake Tarfala,** a glacial lake with turquoise waters. What makes the water this colour? Glaciers act like bulldozers, crushing rocks as they travel along valley floors. These rocks become a fine powder, which is deposited in lakes like this one. When sunlight hits the lake, the water looks bluish-green.

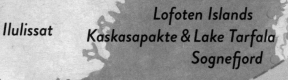

Norway is known as the land of the fjords. It has more than 1,000 of them. These narrow, long inlets of the sea were created by the movement of glaciers. **Sognefjord** is Norway's longest and deepest fjord. You'd have to go down 4,291 feet (1,308 meters) to reach the bottom!

Located north of the Arctic Circle, the **Lofoten Islands** are off Norway's northwestern coast. People from all around the globe come here to surf, despite the sea ice and ice-cold waters.

Northern Canada's **Ellesmere Island** is home to several ice shelves. These thick ice slabs connect to the island along its coastline.

Underneath much of the Arctic is permanently frozen ground called permafrost. This layer can be up to 3,281 feet (1,000 meters) thick. As the Earth's climate warms, some of the Arctic's permafrost is thawing. This can lead to landslides or cause the ground to collapse, forming craters like this one in **Siberia**.

The Arctic is home to the world's biggest island, Greenland, which has far more ice than greenery, despite its name. On the island's west coast is the town of **Ilulissat**, known as the iceberg capital of the world because thousands of icebergs are produced by a nearby glacier. People sail, hike, or see them by taking flights over the area. Ilulissat is home to about 4,530 people and almost as many sled dogs: 3,500!

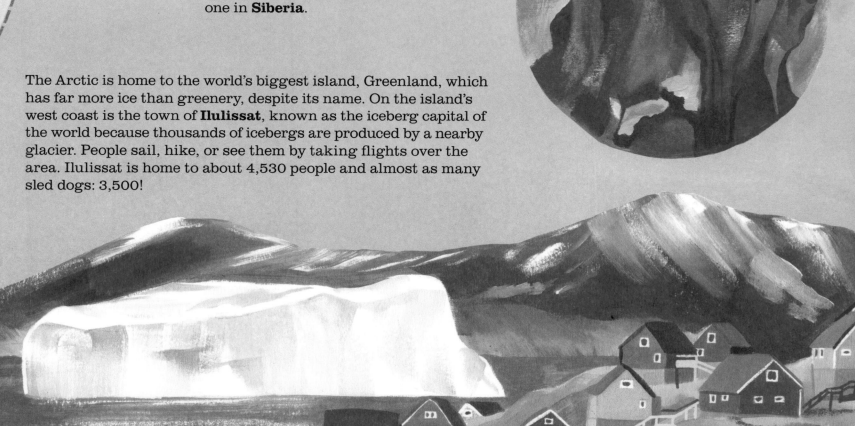

SHRINKING SEA ICE

Global warming is causing rapid changes in the polar regions' sea ice and has been shrinking rapidly in recent decades.

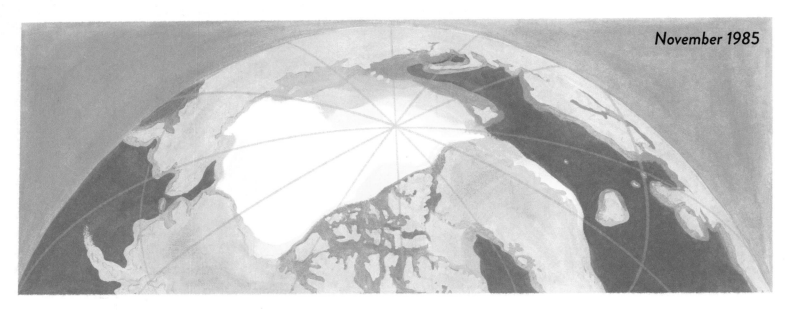

November 1985

The picture above shows the extent of Arctic sea ice in November 1985. The whiter the color, the thicker the ice sheet.

The one below shows its extent in November 2018—quite a difference!

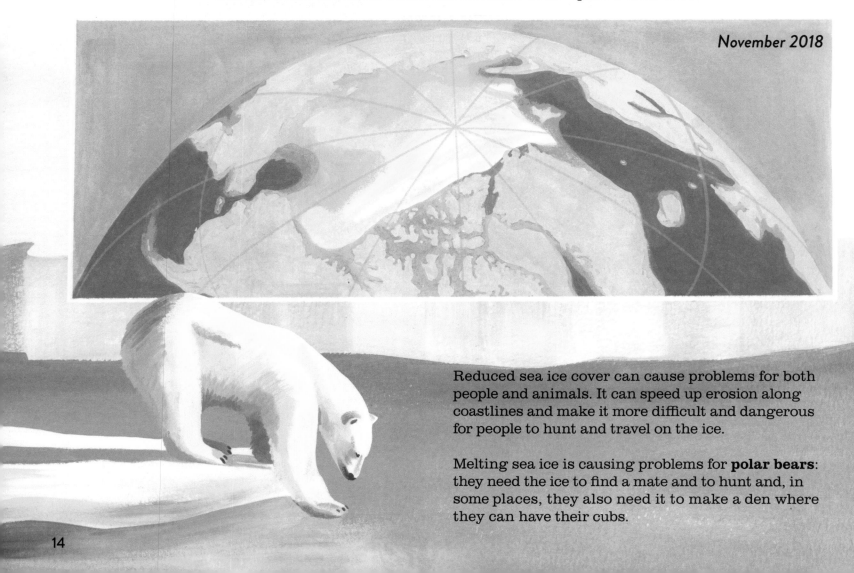

November 2018

Reduced sea ice cover can cause problems for both people and animals. It can speed up erosion along coastlines and make it more difficult and dangerous for people to hunt and travel on the ice.

Melting sea ice is causing problems for **polar bears**: they need the ice to find a mate and to hunt and, in some places, they also need it to make a den where they can have their cubs.

During the winter, sea ice forms in the Arctic and Antarctic regions. This frozen seawater floats on the surface of the ocean and, for the most part, melts in the summer. However, some sea ice remains all year round in certain places—in fact, it covers roughly 15 percent of the world's oceans during some of the year.

Sea ice affects the **global climate**. How? The white surface of sea ice reflects way more sunlight back than ocean water does. As sea ice melts, more of the darker ocean water is exposed. This darker water absorbs more sunlight, which makes temperatures rise, causing even more ice to melt. Over time, this cycle can cause global climate change.

Our ecosystem is connected very closely and climate change is affecting a number of Antarctic species. The population of **Adélie penguins** is shrinking. What does this have to do with the melting of the ice?

It is suspected that global warming affects the breaking of the thick ice sheets in Antarctica. This can also create new icebergs.

Adélie penguins depend on krill for food, which normally feed on **algae** found on the underside of the sea ice. The West Antarctic Peninsula has lost a significant amount of sea ice.

Less sea ice means less algae for the **krill** to eat, which results in a declining krill population.

This means less food for Adélie penguins, and they ultimately struggle to survive.

THE DARK NIGHT

Each year, both poles experience one very long day, polar day, and one very long night, polar night.

Polar regions experience extremes of daylight and darkness because of the tilt of Earth's axis as it spins. The extremes of polar day and night grow as one gets closer to the poles.

June 21

In June, it's summer in the Arctic and winter in Antarctica.

Here is the Antarctic experiencing **polar night**. The southern hemisphere is tilted away from the Sun during this time. At Halley VI Research Station, on the Brunt Ice Shelf in Antarctica, there is 24-hour darkness for 105 days each year. It's dark all the time, even at 11 am.

On **Midwinter's Day** (June 21), people at many Antarctic research stations have big celebrations. They often exchange presents and have a special feast. Some get breakfast in bed and some even do a polar plunge, where they dive—sometimes naked!— into the seawater through a precut hole in the ice. The temperature of the water is typically about 28.4°F (-2°C)!

The Antarctic

Tromsø, Norway, is located more than 200 miles (300 kilometers) north of the Arctic Circle. Here, polar day lasts from May to July, but it carries on for much longer at the north pole.

The Arctic

Tromsø

23:00

June 21

As the Earth travels around the **Sun**, Antarctica and the Arctic receive different amounts of sunlight, depending on the time of year.

When it's **polar day** in the Arctic, people can kayak and bike in daylight, even at 11 pm. During this time of year, the northern hemisphere is tilted toward the Sun, which doesn't set.

The extremes of light and darkness affect animals in many ways. The color of reindeer eyes changes with the seasons for example. When there's 24-hour darkness, their eyes are blue, but when it's light all the time their eyes are golden. When their eyes are blue they are more sensitive to light, which means they can see more in winter, but their vision is not as sharp.

NATURE'S FIREWORKS

During the long nights, you can observe colorful spectacles of auroras in the skies over the Arctic and Antarctic.

When throwing off their incredible light shows, auroras also make sounds. These noises have been described as a surging hiss, muffled banging, sputters, or crackles.

An old Finnish folk tale says that auroras are caused when foxes run over the snow, their tails causing sparks to be sent way up into the sky as they brush the surface. Storytelling is often an important part of Arctic peoples' cultures. Many indigenous groups have their own legends about what causes them. Some of these say they are the torches of sky giants, others that the lights are powerful spirits.

Auroras are shimmery, colorful lights that occur high up in the sky. They happen when very small electrically charged particles from the Sun mix with gases in the Earth's atmosphere, causing the particles to glow. Auroras can only be seen at night and are often best viewed near the equinoxes in March and September, typically the hours around midnight.

They come in a variety of colors, including green, pink, red, violet, and blue. Sometimes auroras look like curtains made of light. They can have a band-like shape or break into small arcs.

People can see auroras in both polar regions. In the northern hermisphere, they are called aurora borealis; in the southern hemisphere, they're known as aurora australis. Aurora was the Roman goddess of the dawn.

ROUGH JOURNEYS

Who were the first brave humans to encounter the southern end of the world? Throughout history, explorers have shown courage and creativity when facing the many challenges of the continent.

Though an essential part of hundreds of expeditions, sled dogs have been banned from Antarctica since 1994. The dogs might transfer diseases to the native seal population and disturb the wildlife.

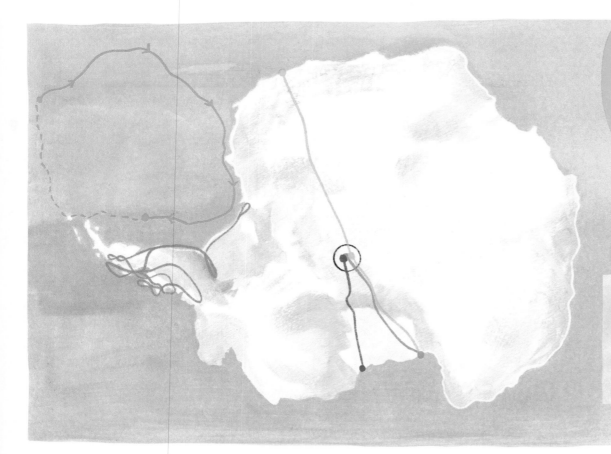

- Robert Falcon Scott
- Roald Amundsen
- Ernest Shackleton
- Finn and Edith Ronne
- Ann Bancroft & Liv Arnesen

Robert Falcon Scott commanded two expeditions to the Antarctic in the early 1900s. His teams discovered much about the oceanography, climate, and past animal and plant life in the region. Although he was not the first to reach the south pole, he was a hugely successful explorer! Sadly, after reaching the south pole in January 1912, he and four team members died in Antarctica of ailments including malnutrition and exposure.

In December 1911, **Roald Amundsen** became the first explorer to reach the south pole. His team members were excellent at skiing fast, navigating across Antarctica's challenging landscape, and running dogsleds. The expedition relied heavily on well-trained Greenland dogs to pull their sleds. Amundsen's crew wore more fur clothes than Scott's crew did and sat on cold sleds, while Scott's team manhauled theirs, which made them hot.

Originally, the goal of **Ernest Shackleton**'s 1914–16 expedition was to cross Antarctica via the south pole. Unfortunately, his ship, Endurance, became trapped in the ice of the Weddell Sea in early 1915. Shackleton and his crew—including the resident cat, Mrs. Chippy—didn't give up. The men played games on the ice, had races with the dogs, held singalongs in the evenings, and observed the wildlife and the stars. In October, ice squeezing against the ship caused it to start breaking up and water to pour in, so the crew abandoned it and set up camp on the ice. The Endurance finally sank in November. Shackleton and his men were rescued in 1916.

Endurance's crew members even built dog igloos—called dogloos—from ice and wood so the dogs had somewhere to sleep on the ice.

Mapping and exploring the Weddell Sea coastline was a huge accomplishment of **Finn Ronne**'s 1947–48 expedition. His team took about 14,000 aerial photographs of the region. Ronne's wife **Edith** worked as a scientist and journalist on the expedition. She was also the first American woman to set foot on the Antarctic continent. Their expedition's work showed that Antarctica was one continent rather than two separate islands.

In 2001, **Ann Bancroft** and **Liv Arnesen** became the first women to ski across Antarctica. Before their expedition, they trained in unusual ways: They pulled tires attached to their waists along gravel roads. They ran up cliffs while carrying backpacks full of cat litter. They even tested communications equipment inside a huge ice-cream freezer.

Bancroft and Arnesen skied and wind-sailed all while pulling 250-pound (113-kilogram) sleds behind them!

PROVEN SURVIVAL SKILLS 🐾

At the northern end of the world, Indigenous people helped many Arctic explorers with their expeditions—and their quest for knowledge.

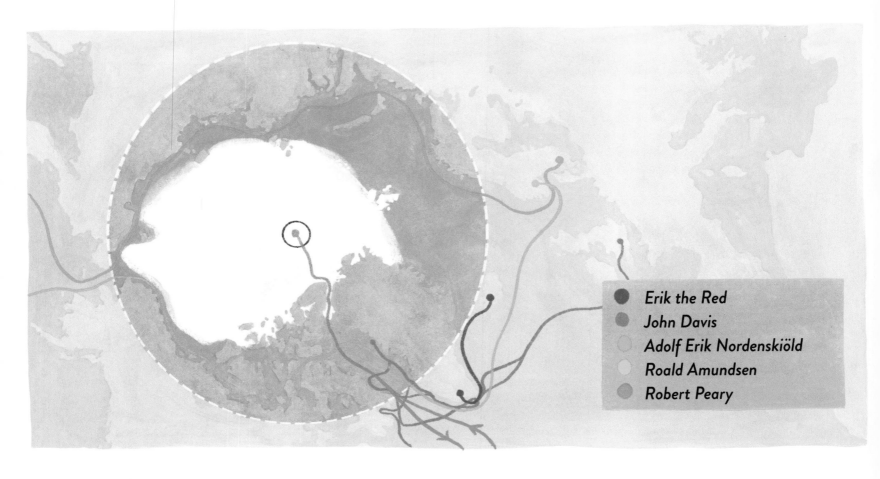

- ● Erik the Red
- ● John Davis
- ○ Adolf Erik Nordenskiöld
- ○ Roald Amundsen
- ● Robert Peary

In 982, after being exiled from his home in Iceland, the Viking explorer **Erik the Red** headed west, to Greenland. He traveled by *knörr* (or *knarr*), a type of ship that had both sails and oars, and gave this land its name and explored much of it and its surrounding islands and coastline. He also established Greenland's first European settlement.

John Davis led three Arctic expeditions between 1585 and 1587. One of his expedition teams included four musicians, who played for local Inuit people they met on Greenland's coast. The two groups danced together and the Inuit brought drums to share their music, too. Davis gave the world much new information about the plants, geology, and weather of the Arctic. He also gathered data on much of the region's uncharted coastline.

In 1878–79, the explorer and scientist **Adolf Erik Nordenskiöld** became the first to successfully navigate the Northeast Passage. This maritime route goes through the Arctic, mainly along Siberia's northern coast. Nordenskiöld's team members collected starfish and marine algae from the bottom of the ocean, photographed the people and landscapes they encountered, and made maps of the Norwegian island of Spitsbergen and Siberia's northern coast.

Their daily food ration included lime juice to prevent scurvy.

In addition to navigating the Northwest Passage by boat, **Roald Amundsen** spent almost two years of his 1903–06 expedition on King William Island, in what is now Nunavut. Here, the indigenous people taught Amundsen's team survival skills, such as how to make igloos quickly, drive dogs, and dress warmly enough (loose fur clothing is key).

Robert Peary had 40 dogs and just five human companions for the final 134 miles (216 kilometers) of his 1909 expedition to the north pole. Four were Inuit men (named Ooqeah, Ootah, Egingwah, and Seeglo). The fifth was Matthew Henson, an African-American explorer who spoke the Inuit language and was a fantastically skilled hunter, dog handler, carpenter, and fisherman. Henson was said to have actually been the first to reach the north pole. However, scholars today believe that while Peary's team got close to the pole, they didn't actually make it to its exact location.

September 2019 saw the launch of the **MOSAiC expedition**, when the icebreaker Polarstern left Tromsø and headed for the Arctic Ocean to spend a year drifting in the ice near the north pole. Supported by hundreds of researchers from 20 countries, the team is studying the effects of climate change.

Scientists on the MOSAiC mission look overboard at the bioluminescent creatures in the ocean below their ship. The bodies of these organisms (likely marine plankton) give off light.

WHO LIVES HERE?

Many indigenous groups make their homes in the Arctic, each with its own culture. Some even take a snowmobile to school!

Aleut   Chukchi   Evenk   Inuit   Khanty Nenets   Sámi   Yupik

Indigenous peoples have lived in the Arctic for thousands of years. It's estimated that roughly 10 percent of the people who live in Arctic areas are indigenous and the region is home to more than 40 different groups, some of whom are pictured above.

Just like in other parts of the world, some Arctic dwellers live in small towns and remote villages. But there are also bigger cities. Murmansk, Russia, lies north of the Arctic Circle and has a population of 300,000.

Several indigenous groups, including the Sámi, have traditionally practiced reindeer husbandry. Today they are more likely to herd their animals while riding on snowmobiles. There are about 80,000 Sámi people spread out across Norway, Sweden, Finland, and Russia, and they support themselves in a variety of ways, from fishing and livestock farming to working in the tourism industry.

24

The Inuit are indigenous people of Canada, Greenland, and Alaska. In the Inuktitut language, the term *Inuit* means "people." Some Inuit still live off the land, hunting, fishing, and trapping animals. Others are involved in mining or tourism. Dogsledding has traditionally been an important part of their culture. Nowadays, many people also choose to use speedier snowmobiles to get around.

About four million people live in the Arctic, but there are no indigenous The people who come to visit this area might be scientists or tourists.

During the school year, Nenets children often attend boarding schools, where they learn about Russian language and culture. They spend the summers with their families migrating across the tundra as they follow their reindeer herds. These animals are essential to the Nenets way of life in Siberia. They are used for food, transportation, and to make shelter and clothing. Reindeer are also a source of income for many Nenets: they earn money by selling the reindeer meat and hides.

FROM FISH TO FLATBREAD

People in the Arctic eat a mixture of foods they hunt and forage for and some that are shipped in from far away.

Dried shrimps

In the Canadian territory of Nunavut, groceries are super-expensive. In 2019, a bunch of grapes cost more than $28 and a package of vanilla cookies cost more than $18!

Imported food

Bannock bread

Musk ox steak

Traditional Inuit foods include **seal meat** and **bannock bread,** which is often cooked in seal oil. **Arctic char,** a popular fish, may be served frozen. **Muktuk,** a treat consisting of whale skin and blubber, is normally eaten raw.

Frozen Arctic char

Raw seal ribs

Muktuk

Dried caribou

Many people consider **suaasat,** or seal soup, to be Greenland's national dish. However, today, traditional and modern foods are often combined, such as seal meat with ketchup or mayonnaise, and all over the Arctic, people are buying more processed foods and drinks, from soda to snack crackers.

Suaasat

Tunnbröd is a flatbread that has been made by the Sámi for centuries. They also collect wild **berries**, including cloudberries and lingonberries. **Hot coffee** is a favorite beverage of theirs.

Berries

Grilled Arctic char

Hot coffee

Reindeer salami

Tunnbröd

Stewed fish and onions

Dried reindeer heart

Reindeer, mashed potatoes, and lingonberries

Dried cod

For the Nenets of the Siberian Arctic, **reindeer meat** is the most important food. Whether raw, frozen, or boiled, it's full of vitamins. Reindeer blood is also a key food source. But in the summer, they depend on fish more because it's tricky to store meat when they are on the move, following their reindeer herds. The Nenets also collect mountain cranberries during summertime.

Reindeer meat and fish such as salmon or arctic char are regular parts of the Sámi diet. Both can be prepared in a variety of ways—dried, salted, smoked, or grilled.

Akutaq

Akutaq is a unique Arctic food. Sometimes known as Eskimo ice cream, it was traditionally made for survival when people went out hunting. There are many different recipes for this hearty treat. Its basic ingredients are typically **caribou** or moose fat; seal, whale, or walrus oil; snow or water; and berries. Today, some cooks add sugar to this amazing Arctic dessert.

HOW TO STAY WARM

Well-designed homes and clothing keep the people of the Arctic warm despite the chilly climate.

Tents made of animal hides are a traditional style of dwelling among many native Arctic peoples. Today, some Sámi *lávut* tents have waxed canvas or other lightweight woven coverings instead of animal hides. Depending on the indigenous group, the tents' support poles could be made of materials ranging from whale-bone to driftwood. Having easy-to-move homes is important when people migrate in search of animal herds such as reindeer.

Chums are the tent homes built by the Nenets of Siberia. Each *chum* normally houses one family and they are big enough inside for normal household activities to take place, such as making clothes, cooking, and taking care of the children.

It is common for Antarctic researchers to learn how people in the Arctic build an igloo in case they need emergency shelter.

A Nenets child outside its chum is dressed in warm clothes made using reindeer fur.

Igloos are dome-shaped structures made from blocks of hard-packed snow. The Inuit often build these temporary shelters in the winter when they are out on hunting trips. Igloos vary in size and can hold up to 20 people inside. An expert igloo maker can build a small one in as little as an hour!

Recent improvements to modern **Arctic homes** include better insulation and heated floors. Some also have special foundations that allow the houses to be easily moved or adjusted if the permafrost below them shifts.

This is one of the family's dogs. The dogs help pull the family's sleds and herd the reindeer.

Throughout the Arctic, men and women wear boots, mittens, pants, and parkas. Native peoples have traditionally made their clothes from furs and animals but, nowadays, lots of Arctic people buy winter clothing made from synthetic materials.

Many Inuit women wear a big furry coat called an **amauti.** It has a large pouch on the back, which is used to carry a small child or infant. The decoration and design of the *amauti* indicate whether its wearer is married, a widow, or an unmarried woman. They also show what region she is from. Inuit mittens are typically made of reindeer fur. Nenets also wear stocking-like boots called **piwa,** which have fur on the outside.

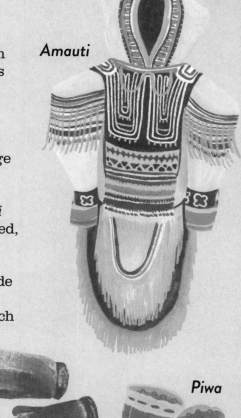

Amauti

Mittens

Piwa

Mal'tsia

The **mal'tsia** is the pullover garment worn by the Nenets. It has mittens and a hood sewn into it and you usually need five or six reindeer skins to create one. Reindeer hide is used on the outside of a coat, while reindeer fur is inside, next to the wearer's skin, to keep them warm.

Even in the chilliest of weather, the furry shoes of the Sámi people, called **nutukkaat,** keep their feet toasty. Reindeer fur, skins, and tendons are all used in the making of traditional clothes and footwear. **Hats** are often made from reindeer-calf pelts.

Hat

Nutukkaat

A RESEARCH STATION

The design of Antarctic research stations varies as much as the research done in them.

Research stations in Antarctica are amazing places. They are designed to meet all the needs of the researchers and staff. Like other homes, they have bedrooms, kitchens, dining rooms, and areas to hang out in or watch TV. And like research facilities around the globe, they have laboratories, meeting rooms, and places to store supplies.

Deliveries of food and equipment are few and far between. Once a year, the icebreaker Polar Star clears a path for a group of supply ships to deliver millions of pounds of cargo and millions of gallons of fuel to McMurdo Station. Most Antarctic researchers come during the summer months.

Antarctica is home to 70 permanent research stations, which are run by 29 different countries.

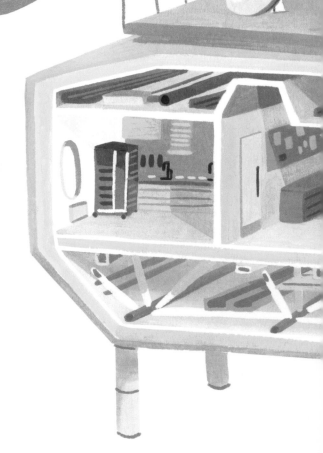

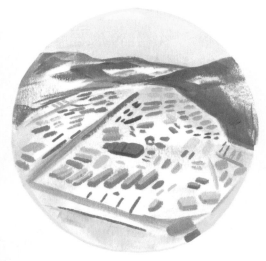

McMurdo Station is the biggest Antarctic research station. In addition to dormitories and science labs, McMurdo has a firehouse, a power plant, warehouses, and stores. It is home to more than 1,200 residents in summer and even has a coffee house and a small cinema!

Jang Bogo Station is a South Korean research station in Antarctica's Terra Nova Bay. This bright blue station is designed to withstand temperatures of -40°F (-40°C) and wind speeds of up to 145 miles (233 kilometers) per hour. So Jang Bogo is a great place to test new equipment, robots, and materials for use in extreme conditions. Research here focuses on meteorites, glaciers, and the ozone layer.

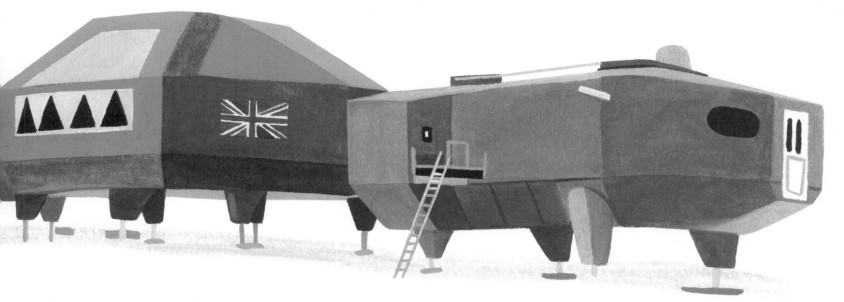

Opened in 2013, the **Halley VI Research Station** is located on Antarctica's Brunt Ice Shelf. It is made up of eight colorful interlinked pods that sit on skis. The European Space Agency has even used this base to help test what it's like to work and live in a very isolated place.

In 2015, two huge cracks appeared in the ice beneath the station, so it was relocated to a new site 14 miles (23 kilometers) further inland. Luckily, the pods can be separated from one another and moved with specialized heavy vehicles.

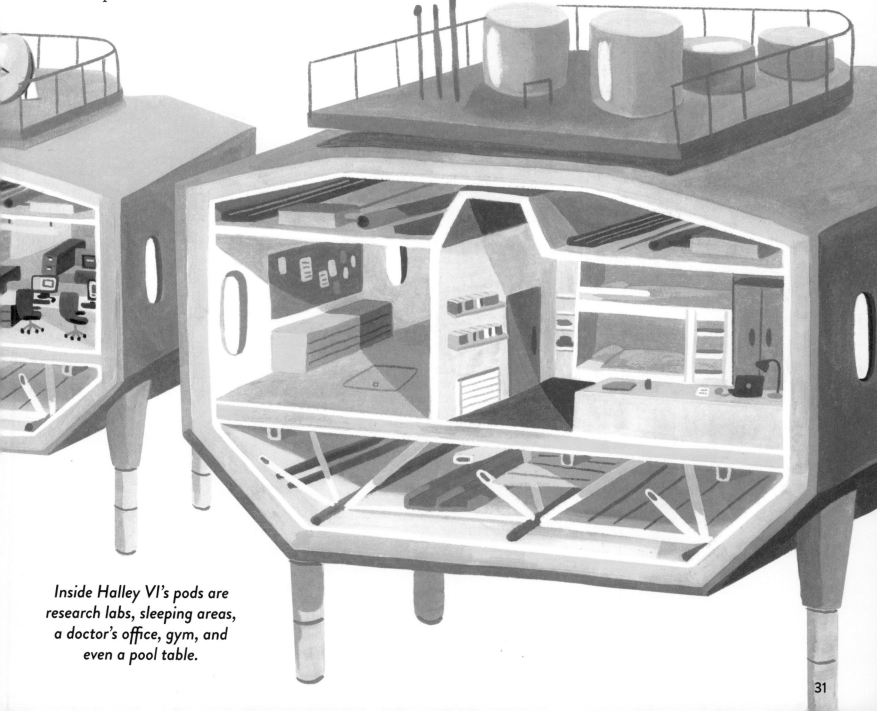

Inside Halley VI's pods are research labs, sleeping areas, a doctor's office, gym, and even a pool table.

A SCIENTIST'S DAY

The days of polar researchers are full of hard work but also fun. Let's follow one through her day of research and relaxation.

Most scientists stay in Antarctica for periods of three to six months. But some stay for up to 15 months (one summer and two winters).

 After gathering equipment from the lab where she works, a polar scientist loads up a Ski-Doo (snowmobile) for the morning ahead. Behind her is a colleague whose Ski-Doo is roped to hers, as it's safer to travel with a partner. These vehicles can zip across the frozen landscape at 50 miles (80 kilometers) per hour. It takes about 45 minutes to arrive at their research site.

Our scientist spends her morning taking measurements of the water's temperature at several locations along the coast. She also collects water samples to bring back to the lab for analysis. She and her partner eat lunch in the field. Peanut butter sandwiches and hot cocoa from a thermos are on the menu.

 The biology lab is a hive of activity all afternoon. Our scientist retrieves the water samples she collected in the morning. She pours a portion of a sample into a beaker to test its chemical composition. After examining the samples, she records the data on her computer.

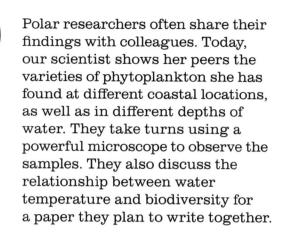

Polar researchers often share their findings with colleagues. Today, our scientist shows her peers the varieties of phytoplankton she has found at different coastal locations, as well as in different depths of water. They take turns using a powerful microscope to observe the samples. They also discuss the relationship between water temperature and biodiversity for a paper they plan to write together.

Exercise is a great way to destress and use up some energy. Some days our scientist runs on a treadmill or lifts weights. But today she spends an hour working out on a climbing wall (Antarctica's McMurdo Station is home to one). After a two-minute shower (a restriction at many polar stations), it's almost dinnertime.

What's cooking tonight? Grilled fish, pasta, tomato soup, falafel. Deliveries of fresh fruit and vegetables are especially rare in Antarctica, so creative chefs largely make appealing meals for polar researchers from canned and dried food. Today, our scientist is not on dishes and cleanup duty, but that's part of life at a research station, too.

Many polar research stations have no trees or grass around them, so reading on a couch inside the station's greenhouse is relaxing and also a boost to our scientist's spirits. The moisture feels nice on her skin and light streams in at all hours during the summertime.

FROM PLASTICS TO POLAR BEARS

Pollution in the Arctic threatens both wildlife and people. Scientists from the Norwegian Polar Institute are studying the impact of microplastics (pieces of plastic smaller than five millimeters) on a seabird called the northern fulmar.

These are all the tiny pieces of plastic inside the fulmar's stomach.

This scientist is getting ready to send up a balloon from Station Nord in Greenland.

A **weather balloon** collects information about the atmosphere. Specifically, it gathers data about pollution and turbulence.

A scientist is putting a coin-size tag onto a polar bear's ear in the Norwegian archipelago called Svalbard. This **tag** will gather information about where the bear is, as well as about the light and temperature in the locations it travels through. The bear has been shot with a tranquilizer dart so it cannot move for an hour or so, then it will return to its normal activities.

Here, the researcher is studying the effects of global warming on insects and other arthropods. The little **plastic greenhouses** increase the temperature inside, which can have a significant impact on how much vegetation the insects eat.

Up to 50 scientists can live and research aboard the **Healy,** a huge ice breaker ship operated by the U.S. Coast Guard. One cool piece of equipment on board is the Van Veen grab, which is a jaw-like tool that can grab samples of sediment and animals from the bottom of the ocean.

The Healy

Not all research projects have people in the field. The Arctic **saildrone** is a surface-water vehicle that is powered by the wind. These saildrones can be used to monitor the seasonal breakup of ice, track marine mammal movement, and measure oceanic conditions.

This saildrone can collect about two million measurements each day, from wind speed to air and water temperatures to chlorophyll concentration and more.

From the land to sea to sky, researchers work on different projects to learn more about polar environments.

The amazing, far-reaching journey of this wandering albatross is tracked, thanks to a **monitor** on its foot. These birds are known to travel as much as 75,000 miles (120,701 kilometers) in a year!

A weather researcher holds up an **anemometer,** a tool used to measure wind speed. The average wind speed at the south pole is 12.3 miles (19.8 kilometers) per hour. But the highest wind speed recorded in Antarctica was 200 miles (327 kilometers) per hour!

Anemometer

Drill

Ice core

A researcher uses a **special drill** to bore down into the ice. This drill allows him to remove a cylindrical **ice core.** An ice core can tell scientists about precipitation, temperature, volcanic activity, and even what the wind patterns were like in the area during different time periods in the past.

Scientists called paleobotanists study **fossil plants** like the one shown here. By analyzing the fossils they find, these experts can discover what plants grew in different sections of Antarctica millions of years ago.

This fossil shows that pine and ginkgo trees grew in Antarctica, as did ferns and other plants.

Antarctic scientists can **drop large nets** from their research vessels into the water. These nets collect a wide variety of plankton specimens, helping us understand more about these creatures and the food web they are a part of.

Plankton

SeaBED is an amazing autonomous vehicle that travels underneath the Antarctic sea ice. It has helped to create 3D maps of the underside of the ice in areas of the Antarctic Peninsula that have been inaccessible in the past.

SeaBED

ANIMALS OF THE ANTARCTIC

The Antarctic is home to a wide variety of wildlife—both in the water and on land.

Despite its seemingly hostile habitat, many organisms are able to survive in the Antarctic. Ribbon worms and sea spiders are just two unique examples that live in the Southern Ocean. In the summer, several whale species, such as humpback whales and orcas, cruise through Antarctic waters. There are even bacteria and algae that live within the ice!

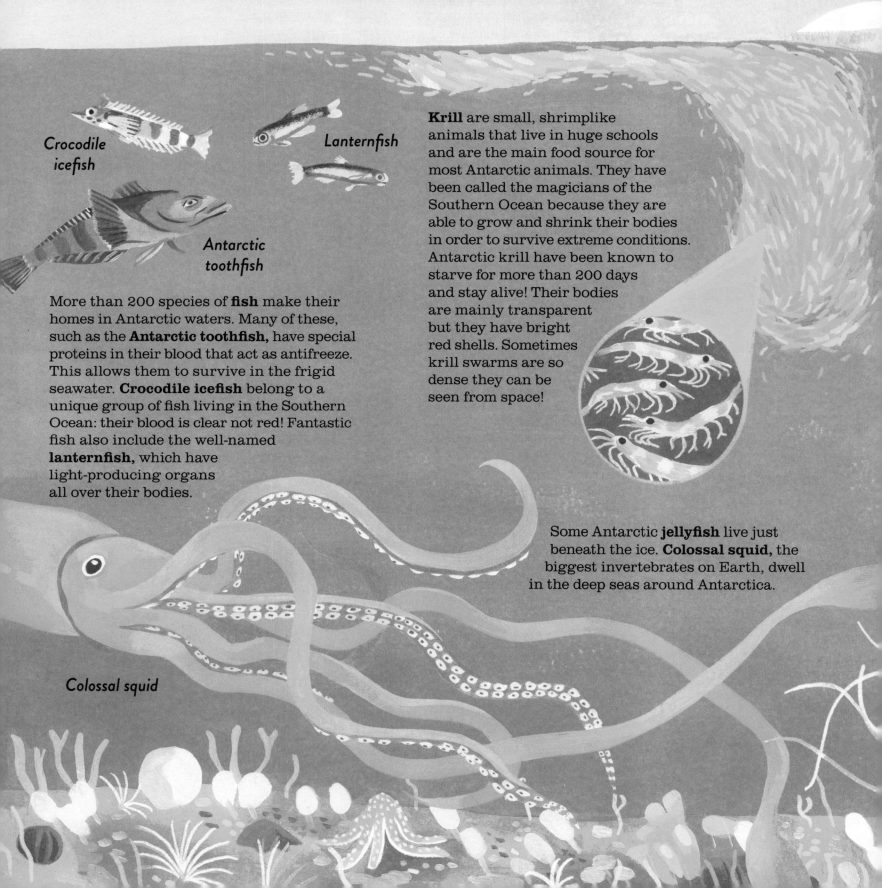

Crocodile icefish

Lanternfish

Antarctic toothfish

More than 200 species of **fish** make their homes in Antarctic waters. Many of these, such as the **Antarctic toothfish,** have special proteins in their blood that act as antifreeze. This allows them to survive in the frigid seawater. **Crocodile icefish** belong to a unique group of fish living in the Southern Ocean: their blood is clear not red! Fantastic fish also include the well-named **lanternfish,** which have light-producing organs all over their bodies.

Krill are small, shrimplike animals that live in huge schools and are the main food source for most Antarctic animals. They have been called the magicians of the Southern Ocean because they are able to grow and shrink their bodies in order to survive extreme conditions. Antarctic krill have been known to starve for more than 200 days and stay alive! Their bodies are mainly transparent but they have bright red shells. Sometimes krill swarms are so dense they can be seen from space!

Some Antarctic **jellyfish** live just beneath the ice. **Colossal squid,** the biggest invertebrates on Earth, dwell in the deep seas around Antarctica.

Colossal squid

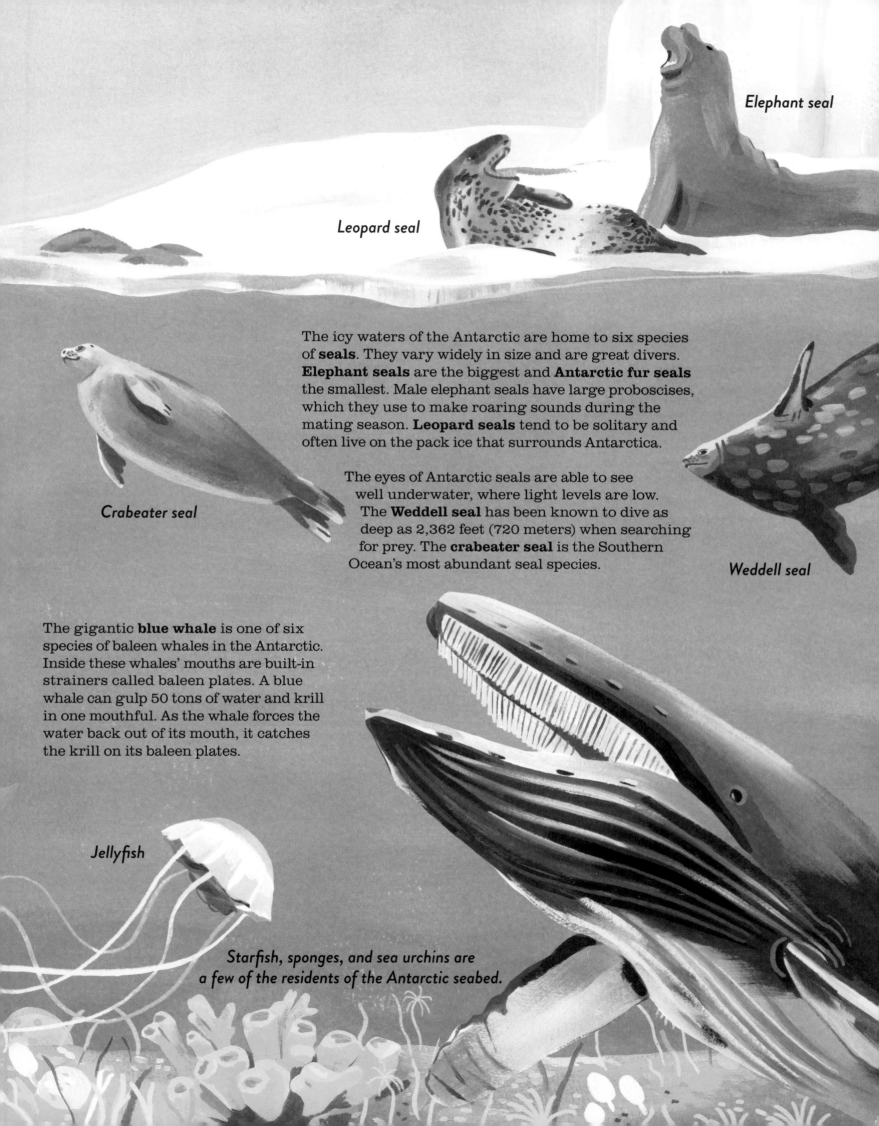

Elephant seal

Leopard seal

The icy waters of the Antarctic are home to six species of **seals**. They vary widely in size and are great divers. **Elephant seals** are the biggest and **Antarctic fur seals** the smallest. Male elephant seals have large proboscises, which they use to make roaring sounds during the mating season. **Leopard seals** tend to be solitary and often live on the pack ice that surrounds Antarctica.

The eyes of Antarctic seals are able to see well underwater, where light levels are low. The **Weddell seal** has been known to dive as deep as 2,362 feet (720 meters) when searching for prey. The **crabeater seal** is the Southern Ocean's most abundant seal species.

Crabeater seal

Weddell seal

The gigantic **blue whale** is one of six species of baleen whales in the Antarctic. Inside these whales' mouths are built-in strainers called baleen plates. A blue whale can gulp 50 tons of water and krill in one mouthful. As the whale forces the water back out of its mouth, it catches the krill on its baleen plates.

Jellyfish

Starfish, sponges, and sea urchins are a few of the residents of the Antarctic seabed.

ANIMALS OF THE ARCTIC 🐾

Many types of animals live in the Arctic—you'll find them on land and in the sea here, too.

The range of animals in the Arctic is just as diverse as the region itself. Mammals range in size from tiny lemmings and weasels to mighty musk oxen and Arctic wolves. Swarms of insects such as mosquitoes and blackflies can blanket the skies. Only three species of whales live year-round in the Arctic: narwhals, belugas, and bowheads.

Seals are other commonly seen Arctic marine mammals.

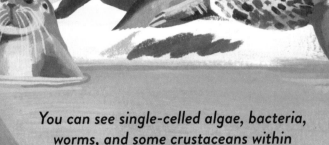

You can see single-celled algae, bacteria, worms, and some crustaceans within Arctic sea ice.

Narwhal

In the north of the United States and Canada, there are even **ice worms**, which spend their entire lives in glaciers. They eat snow algae on the glaciers' surface. If exposed to temperatures just 5 degrees above freezing, these ice worms basically melt and die.

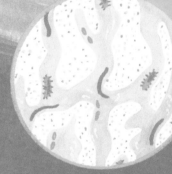

Narwhals, known as the unicorns of the sea, are relatives of dolphins. They live in Arctic rivers and coastal waters. The males have a very prominent tooth that grows into a spiral tusk that can reach up to 10 feet (three meters) in length.

Arctic alligatorfish

Arctic char

Polar cod

Wolffish

Arctic staghorn sculpin

Veteran poacher

Sea lamprey

Arctic skate

Snailfish

Flatfish

Scientists estimate that there are 240 fish species living in the Arctic. The **wolffish** has vertical stripes on its body and a mouth full of powerful teeth, some of which always stick out of its mouth. It can grow to be nearly five feet (1.5 meters) long. The **Arctic char's** color-changing ability is an impressive feature: spawning adults can change from brown to bold orange or red.

Musk oxen and caribou (also called reindeer) are powerful plant eaters. They use their well-designed hooves to dig through the snow as they search for food. They aren't super-picky eaters. They'll chow down on lichens, mosses, roots, grasses, even Arctic summer flowers.

Musk oxen

Caribou

Walrus

Walruses' blubbery bodies keep them comfortable despite their icy-cold water surroundings. Their tusks are perfect for many tasks, such as pulling themselves out of the water, defending their territory, and breaking holes in the ice for breathing. Walruses are very social creatures and lounge around on land in big, loud groups in the summertime.

Belugas

Belugas are social creatures known for their unusual white coloring. They are also known for the extensive range of noises they make, earning them the moniker "canaries of the sea."

Other big Arctic residents are bowhead whales. They are often 50–60 feet (15–18 meters) long and are believed to live for more than 200 years!

Bowhead

Banded gunnel

COPING WITH THE COLD

Animals in polar regions commonly have thick, windproof or waterproof coats. Both reindeer and musk oxen have two **layers of fur**. One is a shorter undercoat next to the skin, the other is a longer layer made up of hollow guard hairs that trap air to keep the animal warm.

Marine mammals, including seals, whales, walruses, and orcas, have a thick layer of fat called **blubber**. It keeps the animals warm in icy-cold waters. The fat can also be an energy store in times of need.

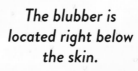

The blubber is located right below the skin.

A penguin's **feathers** keep it warm and dry in the cold ocean waters. But once a year, they molt, and their old feathers get replaced by new ones.

Emperor penguins **gather in huge huddles** to share body warmth and also to shelter them from the wind. They alternate which penguins are on the outside of the huddle. This simple strategy can reduce the animals' heat loss by half.

Many polar animal species, including polar bears and small birds such as Arctic redpolls, stay warm by **curling up into a ball**. Doing this minimizes how much of the animal's body is exposed to the cold.

The extremely cold environments of the Arctic and Antarctic have made it necessary for animals to find ways to adapt. Here is how their bodies and behaviors help them survive!

Seals may warm up by **basking in the sun** on land or ice floes. If they get too hot, they can easily cool off by diving into the chilly waters all around them.

Weddell seals live and breed further south than any other mammal. Their pups are born on the Antarctic ice.

Arctic wolves have adapted in multiple ways. Their **white fur** blends in with their snowy habitat and their ears are smaller than other wolves' ears to help reduce heat loss.

Also, **tufts of fur** between the pads of their feet help them to have a better grip on ice and snow.

Arctic ground squirrels **hibernate** to avoid the extreme winter climate and the lack of available food. Some go into a deep sleep for as long as eight months.

These amazing animals can **drop their body temperatures** to 26.8°F (2.9°C) to save energy. They seem dead but, when the weather gets warmer, they return back to normal.

Since prey is not always abundant, Arctic foxes **hoard food** then store it for later. They might collect birds' eggs or lemmings and cover them with soil, saving them to be enjoyed at a future date.

MASTERS OF THE WATER

Penguins can't fly, but these aquatic birds are able to move easily through the water, ice, and snow of Antarctica.

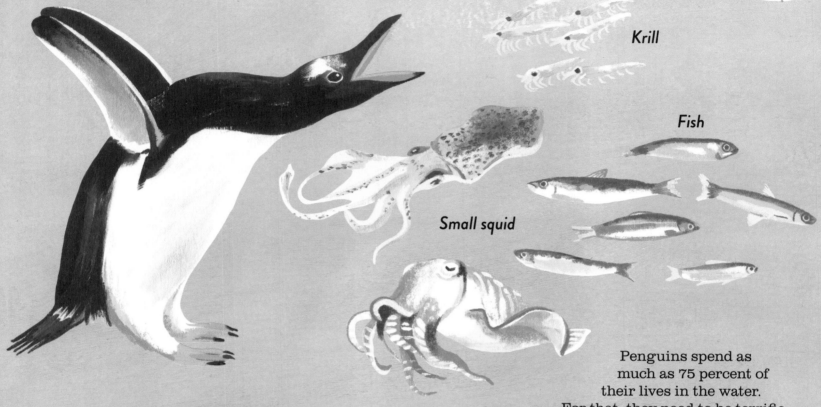

Krill

Fish

Small squid

There are many kinds of seafood on a **penguin's** menu. A main source of food for is krill. They also often eat fish and small squid. Surprisingly, they can eat all of these without teeth! Inside a penguin's mouth are fleshy spines that face backward. These help guide food down its throat.

Penguins spend as much as 75 percent of their lives in the water. For that, they need to be terrific swimmers and incredible divers, which they are thanks to their torpedo-shaped bodies and powerful flippers. They often use a swimming technique called porpoising, where they skim across the water by making multiple consecutive leaps. This lets the penguins move fast and breathe at the surface of the water.

Penguins' coloring works as camouflage, protecting them from predators. From above, they blend in with the dark ocean waters, from below, they look like the brighter ocean surface.

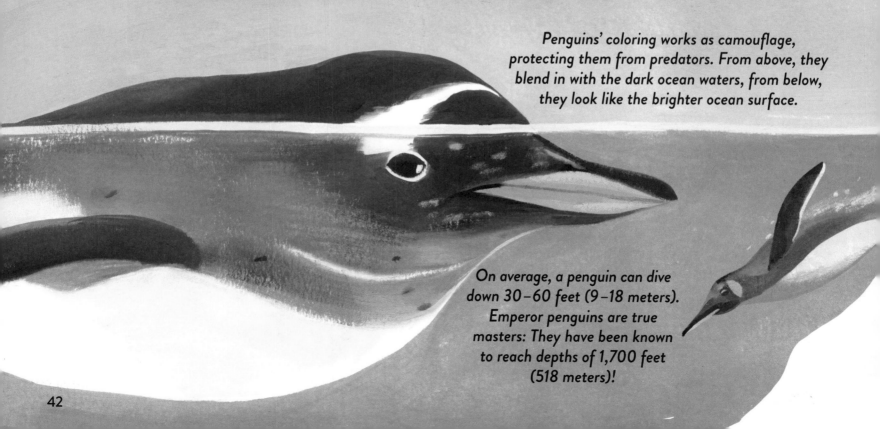

On average, a penguin can dive down 30–60 feet (9–18 meters). Emperor penguins are true masters: They have been known to reach depths of 1,700 feet (518 meters)!

Penguins live in the Antarctic.

Penguins often dive into the water as a group in order to avoid predators, usually leopard seals. Once one penguin dives in, the others follow as quickly as possible.

King

Chinstrap

Macaroni

Rockhopper

Adélie

Gentoo

Magellanic

Emperor

Adélie and emperor penguins are permanent residents of the Antarctic continent. **Chinstrap, gentoo, king, macaroni,** and **rockhopper penguins** live in Antarctic waters, too.

Penguins switch the traditional parental roles around. Once the female penguins have laid their eggs, the males look after them by balancing them on their feet and keeping them warm with a piece of feathered skin called a brood pouch. The males also take care of the chicks once they have hatched, though they become independent after only two to four months. Emperor and king penguins lay only one egg per year, while other species usually lay two.

This chick is about two weeks old.

POWERFUL POLAR BEARS

With their sharp teeth and huge bodies, polar bears are the greatest predators in the Arctic—while also being playful and intelligent.

Polar bears have a great sense of smell. They can sniff a seal that's on the ice from 20 miles (32 kilometers) away!

Polar bears are sensational swimmers. They paddle with their wide front feet and use their hind legs as rudders and, when looking for food, they may swim more than 60 miles (100 kilometers) without resting. They can swim at about six miles (10 kilometers) per hour.

Polar bears have a layer of fat that's two to four inches (five to ten centimeters) thick. This may help them float. It keeps them warm in the freezing air and water of their Arctic home. The fat also gives polar bears an energy store if there are not enough animals to hunt.

When hunting, polar bears are patient. They may stay motionless for hours while waiting for seals to pop out of their breathing holes in the ice.

In the Arctic light, a polar bear's fur can appear to be cream, yellow, or even pink. But underneath their thick fur, polar bears actually have jet black skin!

Ringed seals

The diet of polar bears is mostly made up of seals, **ringed seals** being their main prey. However, they will eat almost anything given the chance, from caribou to birds' eggs to seaweed.

Polar bears only live in the Arctic.

UP IN THE AIR

Birds of all shapes and sizes make
their homes in the polar regions.

The polar regions are popular destinations for a variety
of migratory birds. Why? In the summer, these remote
locations have loads of sunlight and are perfect for
birds that have a short breeding season. In fact, the
Arctic receives more migratory species from around
the globe than anywhere else on Earth!

Skua

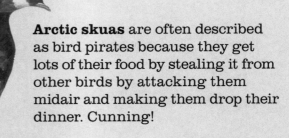

Arctic skuas are often described
as bird pirates because they get
lots of their food by stealing it from
other birds by attacking them
midair and making them drop their
dinner. Cunning!

White-tailed eagle

Snowy owl

A **white-tailed eagle** catches a trout in
its talons. These birds are the biggest in
Greenland. They prey on animals that
range from fish to Arctic foxes to other
birds, including guillemots.

Keen eyesight and hearing help the
snowy owl catch its preferred prey:
lemmings. A single adult snowy owl
can eat more than 1,600 lemmings
in a year.

*The red route shows the Arctic
tern's flight to feed in the Arctic.*

Arctic terns

Arctic terns are frequent fliers. Their
migration is the longest of any animal on
Earth. It's estimated that they travel about
1.49 million miles (2.4 million kilometers from
pole to pole) during their lifetime. Each year
they follow the Arctic and Antarctic summers
and see more daylight than any other animal!
This way, they always have enough food and
avoid their predators like the Arctic fox. Arctic
terns do not fly straight up the center of the
Atlantic Ocean when migrating. Instead, they
often stop in the North Atlantic for a month
to "fuel up" on crustaceans and fish before
crossing the tropics. They travel using a zigzag
route because they follow certain wind patterns
and try to avoid flying directly into the wind.

*The yellow route shows the Arctic tern's
journey to Antarctica between July and
October, to catch the summer down south.*

Wandering albatross

Petrel

There are many varieties of the seabirds called **petrels.** With their long wings, their bodies are well adapted to flying and gliding over open seas.

Every spring, more than 100 million birds breed around Antarctica's rocky coastline and the islands offshore. The **wandering albatross** is the biggest of all seabirds. Their wingspan can measure 11 feet (3.5 meters) and they can soar for great distances without having to flap their wings. In a 10- to 20-day trip, this fantastic flyer can cover 6,213 miles (10,000 kilometers)! They live for a long time—some more than 60 years.

Many kinds of **gulls** live in both the Arctic and Antarctic. Kelp gulls and southern black-backed gulls dwell in the Southern Ocean, hunting and scavenging in flocks. Ross's gulls and Sabine's gulls live in the Arctic all year long. Ross's gulls often breed in remote areas of northern Siberia.

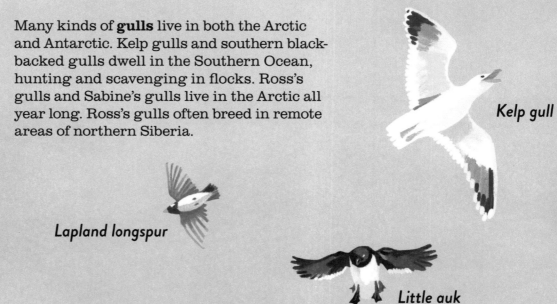
Kelp gull

Razorbill

Lapland longspur

Little auk

Most seabirds need good levels of light to hunt effectively, but scientists discovered that **great cormorants** in Greenland are successful hunters throughout the polar night, often diving for fish in the dark. With their colorful beaks, **puffins** are sometimes called the clowns of the sea, but their diving and fish-catching abilities are no joke. A **rock ptarmigan** is resting on a rock. Its speckled coat shows that it is summertime. In winter, its feathers are all white to match the snow.

Great cormorants

Rock ptarmigan

Puffins

PLANTS' SURVIVAL STRATEGIES

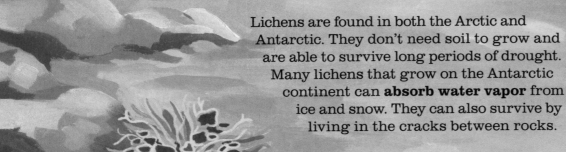

Lichens are found in both the Arctic and Antarctic. They don't need soil to grow and are able to survive long periods of drought. Many lichens that grow on the Antarctic continent can **absorb water vapor** from ice and snow. They can also survive by living in the cracks between rocks.

Colorful **lichens** pop out from icy rocks or grow in the mossy tundra.

Mosses in polar regions can grow even when there's very little sunlight. If conditions are too dry or cold, these plants will go into a **dormant state**. This is a period of very limited activity. The mosses become active when the ice and snow melts again in the summer. Researchers in Canada even managed to bring moss that had been underneath a glacier for 400 years back to life!

Mosses are called "the turtles of the plant world" because they grow so slowly but steadily.

Arctic poppy

The **hairy stem** of the Arctic poppy serves two purposes: it helps trap heat close to the plant and protects it from the wind. The poppy's cup-shaped flowers draw in more sunlight to the center of the flowers, helping them to grow faster. Its flower heads follow the movement of the Sun, which helps the plant maximize how much light it gets to increase photosynthesis.

The snow melts and the soil thaws out as spring turns into summer.

This diagram shows the thawing and freezing cycle of the **active layer of soil** in Alaska's Arctic National Wildlife Refuge. The time frame is roughly from May 15 (far left) to November 15 (far right).

The plants grow well and the active layer has mostly thawed out.

Extreme weather conditions and whipping winds create a harsh environment for plants. To be able to survive in the Arctic and Antarctic they have also had to adapt in unique ways.

Like many polar plants, cotton grass grows close to the ground, helping to protect it from chilly winds. Its **thin leaves** reduce how much water the plant loses through them, while the small seeds of the plant are easily dispersed by the wind and grow quickly once the temperatures warm up.

Cotton grass

Cushion plants

Cushion plants, like many Arctic and Antarctic plants, have a compact design and they **grow close to the ground.** These qualities help the plants survive, despite the wind, snow, and ice. Cushion plants are also able to trap dust in the air, which provides them with a source of nutrients.

Polar plants typically have **shallow roots** located in the unfrozen (or active) layer of soil above the permafrost. When the summer sun heats up the tundra's surface, the uppermost soil thaws out, allowing the roots to grow.

Nodding saxifrage

Alpine foxtail

The soil starts refreezing quickly and the plants stop growing.

ANTARCTICA'S TOUGHEST PLANTS

Even though there isn't a single tree in the Antarctic, hundreds of species of mosses, algae, and lichens are scattered throughout this freezing region. They come in a huge variety and have special features.

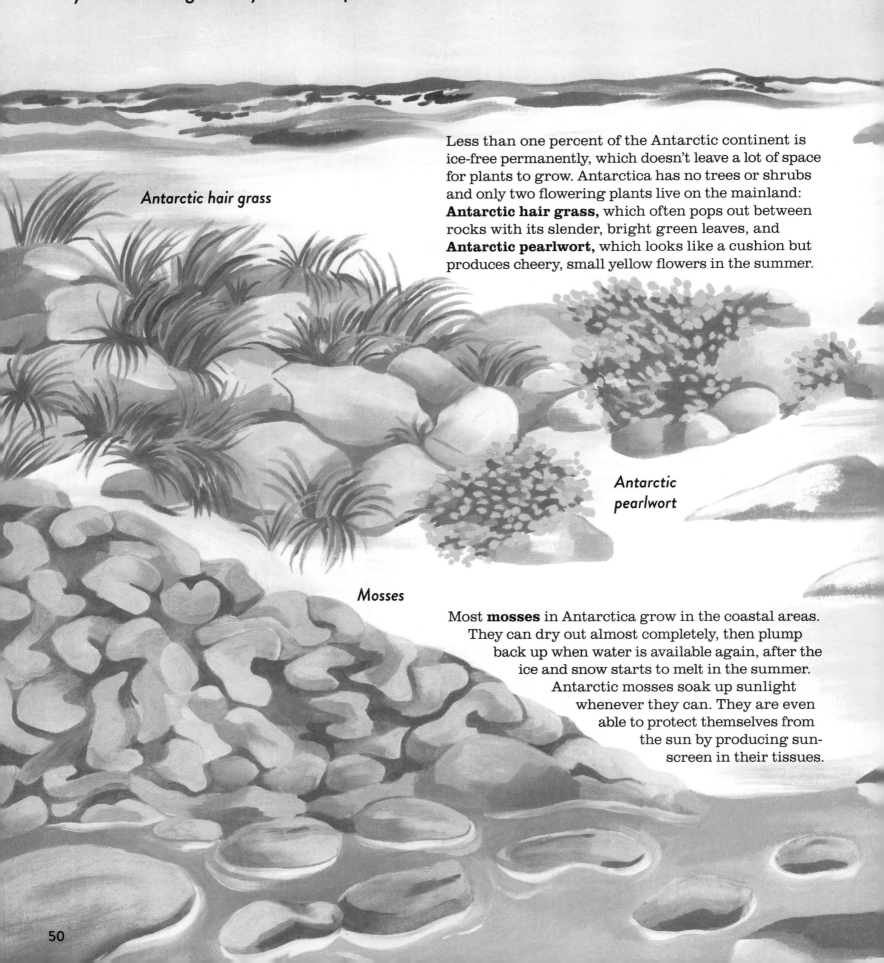

Antarctic hair grass

Mosses

Antarctic pearlwort

Less than one percent of the Antarctic continent is ice-free permanently, which doesn't leave a lot of space for plants to grow. Antarctica has no trees or shrubs and only two flowering plants live on the mainland: **Antarctic hair grass,** which often pops out between rocks with its slender, bright green leaves, and **Antarctic pearlwort,** which looks like a cushion but produces cheery, small yellow flowers in the summer.

Most **mosses** in Antarctica grow in the coastal areas. They can dry out almost completely, then plump back up when water is available again, after the ice and snow starts to melt in the summer. Antarctic mosses soak up sunlight whenever they can. They are even able to protect themselves from the sun by producing sunscreen in their tissues.

Millions of years ago, lush forests covered Antarctica. Scientists have even found pollen from palm trees in the ice.

Red lichens

Antarctic lichens come in many shapes and colors. They are some of the hardiest organisms on Earth and have been found far south. And would you believe that most of their growth happens when they are covered beneath a layer of snow? But lichens don't grow fast: in some parts of Antarctica, it can take 1,000 years for the lichen *Buellia frigida* to grow half an inch (one centimeter).

Orange lichens

Snow algae have adapted to the Antarctic's severe environment. Record-breaking temperatures have caused it to turn some Antarctic snowbanks and snow patches bright red. The red color occurs only when the weather gets warm, as a way of protecting the algae from the sun's UV rays. Even though some researchers call it "watermelon snow" or "raspberry snow," it's not safe to eat.

Snow algae

Scientists recently found foreign **kelp** that had drifted 12,427 miles (20,000 kilometers) into the icy Antarctic waters. As though they were kelp rafts, they had brought "stowaways" with them—other species, including goose barnacles, that could threaten other Antarctic plants or animals.

Kelp

ARCTIC'S MINI PLANTS

The vast area of the Arctic has a huge variety of plant life, from grasses and mosses to lichens and berries in the brightest colors.

Peat moss

Sphagnum moss (or peat moss) commonly grows in the Arctic. Despite their tiny leaves, these plants form a thick, sturdy mat of vegetation when they grow close together. The Inuit in Greenland have used peat moss in porridge and also for medicine. When the scientist Linneaus was traveling in Lapland (a region in northernmost Finland), he made a mattress and blanket to sleep on out of moss!

Sphagnum moss

Arctic lichens grow on rocks or in mat-like structures on the ground. Some have frilly leaves or curvy ones with spots. Others look like cups (**pixie cup lichen**) or even fingers (**Arctic finger lichen**). Lichens range in color from green to orange to black. Caribou often eat them, especially in winter.

Freckle pelt lichen

Pixie cup lichen

Arctic finger lichen

The Arctic tundra is home to roughly 1,700 species of plants. Some lichens are known to be 4,500 years old!

Cottongrass

Pasqueflower

Among the Arctic's plant varieties are shrubs such as Arctic willow and grasslike plants known as sedges. The star-shaped, magenta flowers of the **purple saxifrage** plant add a pop of color to their habitat, often next to snowbanks. Other beautiful blooms include the **pasqueflower** and Arctic parrya.

Purple saxifrage

Arctic poppy

People all over the Arctic pick berries during the summer. **Crowberries** look like blueberries and have been used as food and medicine among the Nenets and Inuit peoples. Bright red **bearberries** are edible but rather flavorless and mealy. Other common berries in this region include lingonberries, **cloudberries,** and **Arctic cranberries.** Known as "the gold of the Arctic," cloudberries contain four times more vitamin C than oranges.

Bearberries

Crowberries

Arctic cranberries

Cloudberries

WHAT A JOURNEY!

You've just completed your first adventure to the polar regions. You've seen jagged mountain peaks, an erupting volcano, and ice in many forms and colors! Amazing animals have crossed your path, both on land and in the ocean. You've seen polar bears and penguins in their natural habitats. You have observed Inuit hunters taking down walruses for their dinner and have snowmobiled alongside Sámi reindeer herders and scientists in the field. You've experienced the midnight sun and the extreme darkness of the polar night.

With your new knowledge of the Arctic and Antarctic regions comes responsibility. It will be your job to help keep these unique environments in good shape for future generations. When you come back, you might listen to indigenous peoples' stories under the colorful northern lights. You might discover new species no one ever knew about before. Or you might even lead your own expedition to the poles in the years to come! Who knows?

GLOSSARY

arthropods: animals without a backbone (such as insects and crustaceans) that have a shell made of a fibrous material called chitin.

chlorophyll: a green pigment found in all green plants that is needed for the process of photosynthesis.

dormant: relating to a period when growth or other biological activity is greatly reduced or suspended.

erosion: the process of being worn away, such as by wind or water.

expeditions: voyages or journeys undertaken by a group of people, especially for exploration or scientific research.

geology: a science describing the structure of the Earth and what's beneath its surface.

glacier: a large mass of ice that moves slowly down a valley or slope, or that spreads outward over a land surface.

icebergs: large floating ice masses that have detached from a glacier.

ice floes: sheets of floating ice.

ice sheet: a mass of ice covering a huge territory – more than 50,000km2!

ice shelf: a sheet of ice floating on the water's surface, that's still connected to a glacier **or** a coastline.

indigenous: native; originating in a particular location or place.

invertebrates: animals that do not have a backbone.

kelp: any of a variety of large brown seaweed.

lichens: simple, slow-growing plants that often form crust-like or leaflike growths on rocks or trees.

pack ice: an area of sea ice floating on the ocean surface.

permafrost: a permanently frozen layer of soil beneath the surface, mainly occurring in polar regions.

photosynthesis: the process by which plants and some other organisms use sunlight to make oxygen and sugar.

plankton: tiny floating or weakly swimming organisms living in the ocean or fresh water.

spawning: releasing or fertilizing eggs, or producing young.

species: a category of living things made up of related individuals that can produce fertile offspring.

tundra: a landscape where it's too cold for most trees to grow.

turbulence: unsteady movement of water or air.

ALICIA KLEPEIS is an author of more than 100 children's books. Having begun her career at the National Geographic Society, she has expertise in the fields of nature, science, history, geography, and social studies.

GRACE HELMER creates rich, ethereal oil illustrations. Since graduating from Camberwell College of Arts, she has worked with an illustrious list of clients including Apple, Google, *The Washington Post,* and *Vogue.*

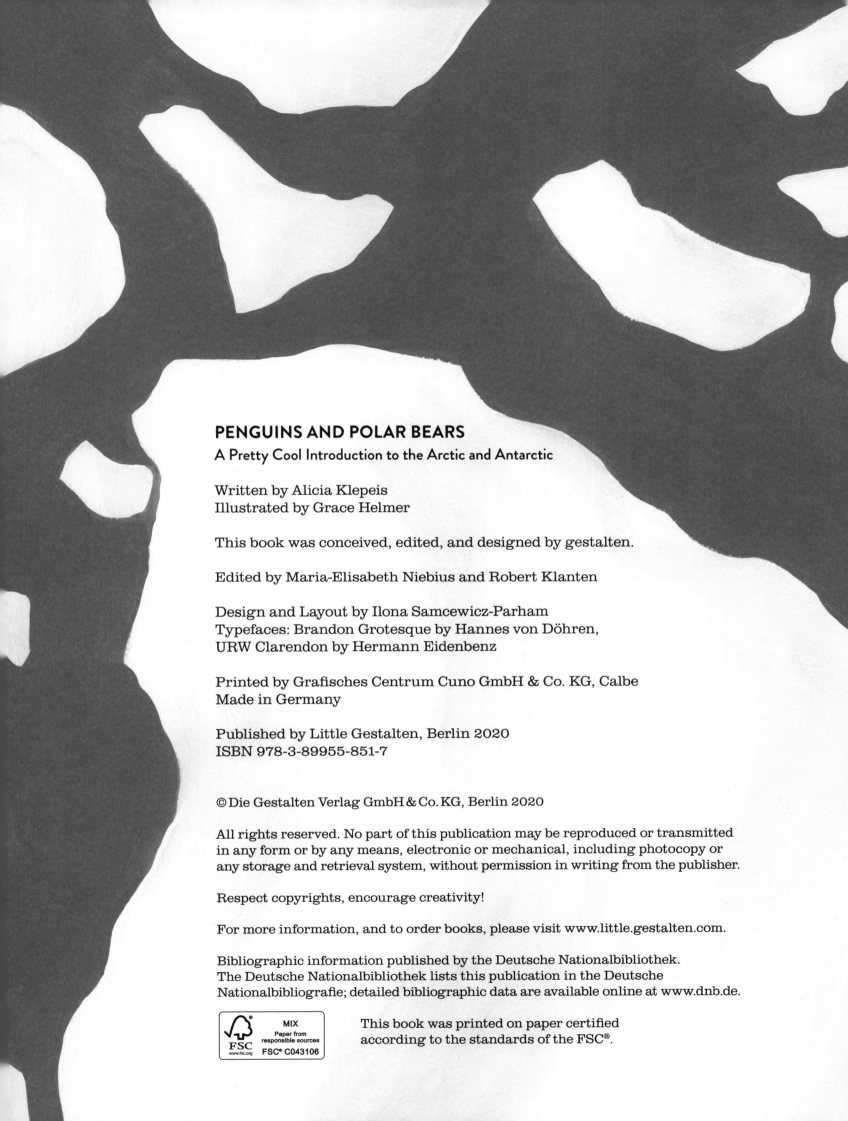

PENGUINS AND POLAR BEARS

A Pretty Cool Introduction to the Arctic and Antarctic

Written by Alicia Klepeis
Illustrated by Grace Helmer

This book was conceived, edited, and designed by gestalten.

Edited by Maria-Elisabeth Niebius and Robert Klanten

Design and Layout by Ilona Samcewicz-Parham
Typefaces: Brandon Grotesque by Hannes von Döhren,
URW Clarendon by Hermann Eidenbenz

Printed by Grafisches Centrum Cuno GmbH & Co. KG, Calbe
Made in Germany

Published by Little Gestalten, Berlin 2020
ISBN 978-3-89955-851-7

© Die Gestalten Verlag GmbH & Co. KG, Berlin 2020

For more information, and to order books, please visit www.little.gestalten.com.

Bibliographic information published by the Deutsche Nationalbibliothek.
The Deutsche Nationalbibliothek lists this publication in the Deutsche
Nationalbibliografie; detailed bibliographic data are available online at www.dnb.de.

This book was printed on paper certified
according to the standards of the FSC®.

FSC
www.fsc.org
MIX
Paper from
responsible sources
FSC® C043106